I Can Name Bills and Coins

Rebecca Wingard-Nelson

Enslow Elementary
an imprint of

Enslow Publishers, Inc.
40 Industrial Road
Box 398
Berkeley Heights, NJ 07922
USA

http://www.enslow.com

Need More Practice?
Free worksheets available at
http://www.enslow.com

CONTENTS

Coins and Bills

one-dollar bill
$1

five-dollar bill
$5

ten-dollar bill
$10

twenty-dollar bill
$20

penny
1¢

nickel
5¢

dime
10¢

quarter
25¢

3

What Is Money?

Coins and bills are kinds of money.

Coins are made from metals, such as copper and nickel.

Bills are made of paper and cloth, such as cotton and linen.

How Is Money Used?

People do work to earn money.

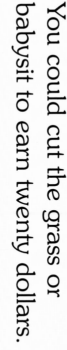

You could cut the grass or babysit to earn twenty dollars.

People use money to pay for things, such as food, clothes, and haircuts.

You could buy a new hat for twenty dollars.

What Is a Penny?

This is a penny.

front of
a penny

President Abraham Lincoln is on the front of the penny.

A penny is worth one cent.
One cent is written as 1¢, or $0.01.

back of
a penny

What Is a Nickel?

This is a nickel.

front of
a nickel

President Thomas Jefferson is on the front of the nickel.

A nickel is worth five cents.

Five cents is written as 5¢, or $0.05.

back of
a nickel

What Is a Dime?

This is a dime.

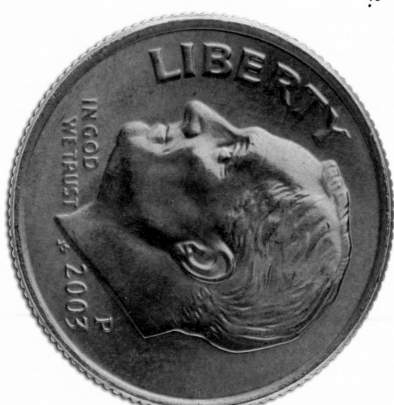

front of
a dime

President Franklin Delano Roosevelt is on the front of the dime.

A dime is worth ten cents.

Ten cents is written as 10¢, or $0.10.

back of
a dime

What Is a Quarter?

This a quarter.

front of
a quarter

President George Washington is on the front of the quarter.

A quarter is worth twenty-five cents.
Twenty-five cents is written as 25¢, or $0.25.

An eagle is usually on
the back of the quarter.

back of
a quarter

Some quarters have special designs on the back.
There is a quarter for each of the 50 states.

What Do Bills Look Like?

This is a one-dollar bill.

front of a dollar

President George Washington is on the front of the one-dollar bill.

A one-dollar bill is worth one dollar, or 100 cents. One dollar is written as $1, or $1.00.

There is a "1" in each corner. It tells you how much the bill is worth.

back of a dollar

What Are Some Other Bills?

This is a five-dollar bill. A five-dollar bill is worth five dollars. Five dollars is written as $5, or $5.00.

President Abraham Lincoln is on the front of the five-dollar bill.

A ten-dollar bill is worth ten dollars. Ten dollars is written as $10, or $10.00.

Alexander Hamilton, the first secretary of the treasury, is on the ten-dollar bill.

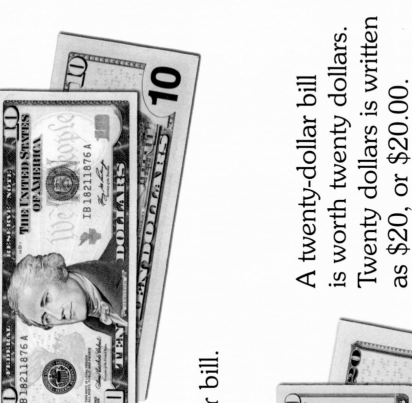

A twenty-dollar bill is worth twenty dollars. Twenty dollars is written as $20, or $20.00.

President Andrew Jackson is on the twenty-dollar bill.

Some Money Combinations

Here are five pennies.
Five pennies are worth 5¢.

A nickel is worth 5¢.

5¢   =   5¢

Five pennies have the same value as one nickel.

Here are five one-dollar bills.
Five one-dollar bills are worth $5.

A five-dollar bill is worth $5.

$5

$5

=

Five one-dollar bills have the same value
as one five-dollar bill.

LET'S REVIEW

1. What coin is this?
   How much is it worth?

2. What coin is this?
   How much is it worth?

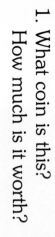

3. What bill is this?
   How much is it worth?

4. What bill is this?
   How much is it worth?

5. What coin is this?
   How much is it worth?

6. What coin is this?
   How much is it worth?

7. What bill is this?
   How much is it worth?

8. What bill is this?
   How much is it worth?

22

1. a penny, 1¢; 2. a dime, 10¢; 3. a one-dollar bill, $1.00;
4. a ten-dollar bill, $10.00; 5. a nickel, 5¢; 6. a quarter, 25¢;
7. a five-dollar bill, $5.00; 8. a twenty-dollar bill, $20.00

LEARN MORE

Books

Cooper, Jason. *American Coins and Bills.* Vero Beach, Fla.: Rourke Publishing, 2003.

Hill, Mary. *Dollars.* New York: Children's Press, 2005.

Roverson, Erin. *All About Money.* New York: Children's Press, 2004.

Web Sites

H.I.P. Pocket Change.
<http://www.usmint.gov/kids/>

U.S. Treasury–For Kids.
<http://www.ustreas.gov/kids/>

23

INDEX

Enslow Elementary, an imprint of Enslow Publishers, Inc.

Enslow Elementary® is a registered trademark of Enslow Publishers, Inc.

Library of Congress Cataloging-in-Publication Data

Wingard-Nelson, Rebecca.
I can name bills and coins/ Rebecca Wingard-Nelson.
    p. cm.—(I like money math!)
Includes bibliographical references and index.
Summary: "An introduction to money for young readers, with pictures, names, and values of American currency"—Provided by publisher.
ISBN-13: 978-0-7660-3140-1
ISBN-10: 0-7660-3140-3
1. Money—United States—Juvenile literature. 2. Paper money—United States—Juvenile literature. I. Title.
HG501.W7 2010
332.4'973—dc22

2008050075

ISBN-13: 978-0-7660-3660-4 (paperback)
ISBN-10: 0-7660-3660-X (paperback)

Printed in the United States of America

10 9 8 7 6 5 4 3 2 1

To Our Readers: We have done our best to make sure all Internet Addresses in this book were active and appropriate when we went to press. However, the author and the publisher have no control over and assume no liability for the material available on those Internet sites or on other Web sites they may link to. Any comments or suggestions can be sent by e-mail to comments@enslow.com or to the address on the back cover.

Photo Credits: © Photos.com, pp. 6, 7; © Shutterstock, pp. 3, 4, 5, 6, 7, 10, 11, 12, 13, 14, 15, 16, 20, 21, 22

Cover Photo: Shutterstock

Enslow Publishers, Inc.
40 Industrial Road
Box 398
Berkeley Heights, NJ 07922
USA

Enslow Elementary
an imprint of

PO Box 38
Aldershot
Hants GU12 6BP
UK

http://www.enslow.com